CRABTREE
CONTACT

JUNGLE SURVIVAL GUIDE

Ruth Owen

In the Amazon rain forest

 Crabtree Publishing Company

www.crabtreebooks.com

Crabtree Publishing Company

www.crabtreebooks.com

1-800-387-7650

PMB 59051
350 Fifth Avenue, 59th Floor
New York, NY, 10118

616 Welland Avenue,
St. Catharines, Ontario
L2M 5V6

Content development by
Shakespeare Squared

Published by
Crabtree Publishing
Company © 2010

www.ShakespeareSquared.com

First published
in Great Britain in
2010 by TickTock
Entertainment Ltd.

Printed in the
U.S.A./122009
CG20091120

Crabtree Publishing
Company credits:
Project manager: Kathy Middleton
Editor: Reagan Miller
Proofreader: Crystal Sikkens
Production coordinator: Katherine Berti
Prepress technician: Katherine Berti

TickTock credits:
Publisher: Melissa Fairley
Art director: Faith Booker
Editor: Emma Dods
Designer: Emma Randall
Production controller: Ed Green
Production manager: Suzy Kelly

Thank you to Lorraine Petersen and the members of nasen

Picture credits (t=top; b=bottom; c=centre; l=left; r=right; OFC=outside front cover; OBC=
outside back cover): Arco Images GmbH/Alamy: 20-21. John Clegg/ardea.com: 7b. Michael
Doolittle/Alamy: 19. Eye Ubiquitous/Alamy: 29b. Monalyn Gracia/Corbis: 8t. iStock: 2, 12tr,
12c, 12b, 14, 18bl, 22, 28t, 31cr. John Giustina/Getty Images: 15. Wolfgang Kaehler/Corbis: 6t.
Robb Kendrick/Getty Images: 18bc. NHPA/Bill Love: 21b. Gerd Ludwig/Corbis: 6t. NHPA/Ma
Bowler: 10t. Photo 24/Getty Images: 23. Photodisc/Getty Images: 26–27. Paul Raffaele/Rex
Features: 29t. Shutterstock: OFC, 1, 4, 5, 7t, 7c, 8b (both), 9, 11t, 11c, 12tl, 13 (both), 16–17
(all), 18t, 18br, 24, 25, 28b, 31t (x3), 31cl, 3c, OBC. www.janespencer.com: 9t, 10b, 11b.

Every effort has been made to trace copyright holders, and we apologize in advance
for any omissions. We would be pleased to insert the appropriate acknowledgments
in any subsequent edition of this publication.

Library and Archives Canada Cataloguing in Publication

Owen, Ruth, 1967-
      Jungle survival guide / Ruth Owen.

(Crabtree contact)
Includes index.
ISBN 978-0-7787-7533-1 (bound).--ISBN 978-0-7787-7555-3 (pbk.)

            1. Jungle survival--Juvenile literature. I. Title.
III. Series: Crabtree contact

GV200.5.O943 2010   j613.6'909152   C2009-906791-9

Library of Congress Cataloging-in-Publication Data

Owen, Ruth.
   Jungle survival guide / Ruth Owen.
      p. cm. -- (Crabtree contact)
   Includes index.
   ISBN 978-0-7787-7555-3 (pbk. : alk. paper)
   -- ISBN 978-0-7787-7533-1 (reinforced library binding : alk. paper)
   1. Jungle survival--Juvenile literature. I. Title. II. Series.

GV200.5.O94 2010
613.6'9--dc22

2009047090

CONTENTS

A Jaguar

CHAPTER 1

LOST IN THE JUNGLE

In your everyday life you have everything you need to survive.

Food comes from a grocery store.
Water comes from a tap.
Your home is warm, dry, and safe.
You do not have to think about survival.

So what would happen if one day all that changed? What would happen if you were flying over a jungle and your plane crashed?

Would you know how to survive in a jungle?

The Amazon rain forest is a huge jungle in South America.

The Amazon rain forest covers more than 2.1 million square miles (5.4 million square kilometers).

In the rain forest, heavy rain falls non-stop for days. You can collect rainwater for drinking in large leaves.

Millions of insects and other animals live in the rain forest. So you will have plenty to eat!

army ant carrying a larva

termite nest

Look under logs for termites, ants, and their **larvae**.

Look in the jungle streams for shrimp.

shrimp

REMEMBER
The basics of survival—water, shelter, and food.

CHAPTER 2

SHELTER

To stay alive, you must build a shelter. A shelter will protect you from the rain.

You will need tools to build a shelter. If you have no equipment, you must **improvise**. This means you must think of new ways to do things.

- A metal belt buckle can become a knife.

- A large rock can be used as a hammer.

Plant stems can be shredded to make fibers. Fibers can be twisted together to make string or rope.

Secure the plant stems with a knot.

Twist both strands clockwise.

Twist one strand around the other.

stem

You will need to find a place to build your shelter.
Find a place that is higher than any nearby rivers.
A sudden flood could wash away your shelter.

rain in the Amazon rain forest

Everything you need to build your shelter is around you.

Tie branches to trees using the string you made from plant fibers.

You can cover your shelter in large leaves.

Imagine waking up to find a million army ants marching through your shelter. You would not want to be sleeping on the ground!

These ants hunt in huge **colonies**. They will eat 50,000 other insects in a day.

army ants

A raised bed will protect you from insects, scorpions, and snakes that could climb on you during the night.

Cover the bed in leaves and grass.

CHAPTER 3 FIRE

You will need a fire for cooking and warmth. When the rain stops, look for a clearing**. Here, the hot Sun will soon dry out materials.**

To build a fire you need tinder, kindling, and fuel.

Tinder is material that will catch fire easily.

Use dry moss or bird feathers for tinder.

Use dry leaves for kindling.

Then you add kindling, which helps the fire burn strongly.

Then you add fuel, which will burn for a long time.

Use bark or broken branches for fuel.

If you do not have matches, you need to make a spark.

Look on the riverbank for **flint** or a sharp-edged rock. Strike the flint with a carbon steel knife. The knife will make a spark.

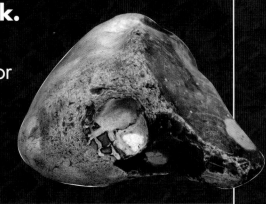

Do not let your fire go out. At night, cover the fire with hot ashes. If you stop air from getting to the fire it will burn very slowly.

In the morning, when you brush away the ashes, the fire will still be burning.

At night, a fire will also protect you...

...from the jaguar.
You may not see him.
But he could be
nearby. Watching YOU.

The jaguar is the world's third largest big cat after tigers and lions. A male jaguar can be nearly 6.5 feet (two meters) long including its tail.

CHAPTER 4

FINDING FOOD

You need food for energy. It also helps to raise your morale. **This means it makes you feel more able to cope with your situation.**

ant

beetle

cricket

termite

Crush ants, beetles, crickets, and termites together to make a tasty paste.

Dig for earthworms
in the leaves and soil.

Eat them raw.

earthworm

Look for birds' nests. Take
one or two eggs to eat.
Mark the other eggs with
charcoal from your fire.

When you go back to the
nest, any eggs without the
mark are freshly laid.

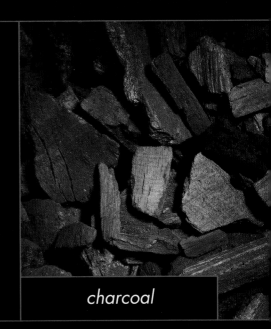

charcoal

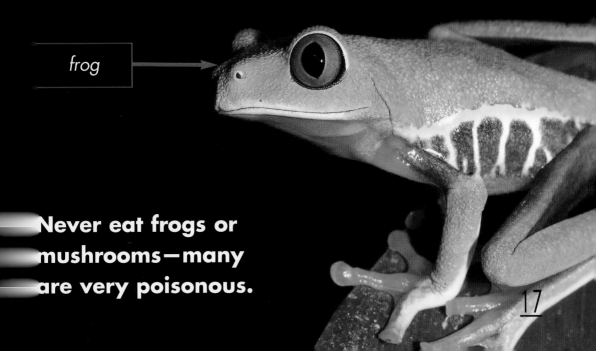

frog

**Never eat frogs or
mushrooms—many
are very poisonous.**

There are many streams and rivers in the Amazon. All freshwater fish are safe to eat. Always boil them or roast them on your fire.

You could make a fishing spear to catch fish. Sharpen a stem of bamboo to make a spear. Stand still in shallow water with the spear point underwater.

Move the point slowly toward a fish. Then, with a sudden push, pin the fish to the riverbed.

bamboo

To make a fishing rod you can improvise. Use your shoelaces as a fishing line. A thorn from a plant can be used as a hook. A worm can be used as bait.

shoelaces

thorn

worms

spear fishing from a canoe

19

CHAPTER 5

JUNGLE DANGERS

**Many dangerous animals live in the Amazon...
...and you are on their** territory**!**

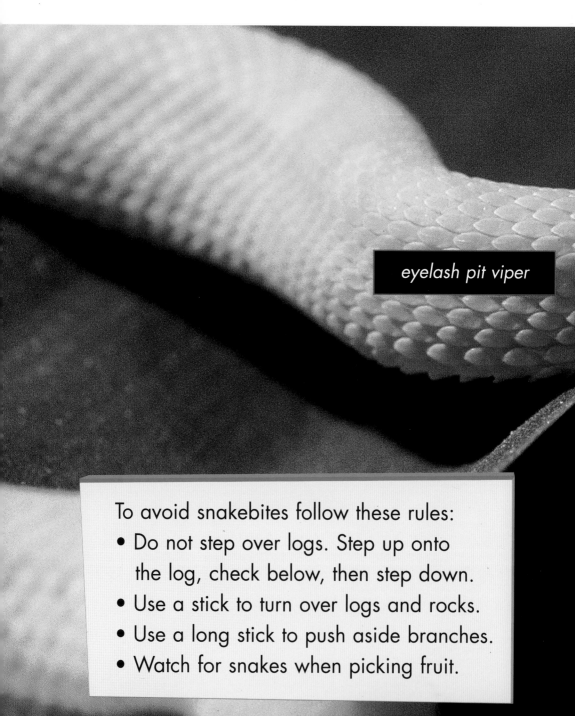

eyelash pit viper

To avoid snakebites follow these rules:
- Do not step over logs. Step up onto the log, check below, then step down.
- Use a stick to turn over logs and rocks.
- Use a long stick to push aside branches.
- Watch for snakes when picking fruit.

You can make a signaling mirror. Anything shiny will catch sunlight and create a flash. The bright flash can attract attention and help you get rescued.

You can even use your belt buckle to make a signal. Always carry it with you in case you hear a plane.

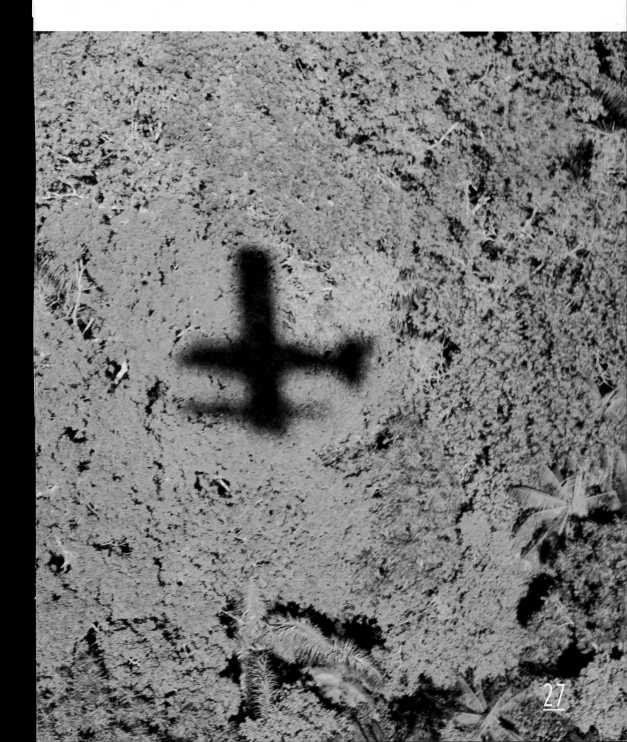

CHAPTER 8

THE SURVIVAL EXPERTS

The Waorani people live in the Amazon in Ecuador. They are experts at jungle survival.

They use blowpipes and poison darts to shoot monkeys for meat.

They add plant poison to river water to stun fish. Then they can catch the fish by hand.

THE SURVIVAL KIT

When you are in a survival situation, it is good to improvise. However, it is better to be prepared. Here are some items that would be good to include in your survival kit.

knife

compass—a tool that tells you which direction you are heading in

whistle to attract rescuers

matches in a waterproof box

flashlight

first-aid kit

Always remember to bring a lot of water.

SURVIVAL ONLINE

Explore a page of Web sites filled with rainforest facts.
www.rain-tree.com/schoolreports.htm

Join film crews, explorers, and scientists in the Amazon rain forest.
www.bbc.co.uk/sn/tvradio/programmes/amazon/index.shtml

Find out more tips and information on jungle survival.
www.storm-crow.co.uk/articles/jungle_survival.html

Publisher's note to educators and parents:
Our editors have carefully reviewed these Web sites to ensure that they are suitable for children. Many Web sites change frequently, however, and we cannot guarantee that a site's future contents will continue to meet our high standards of quality and educational value. Be advised that children should be closely supervised whenever they access the Internet.

INDEX

The Waorani people move from place to place to find food. When they move, they carry their fire in a termite nest. This keeps the fire burning.

blowpipe

Waorani man

NEED-TO-KNOW WORDS

clearing An open area where no trees are growing

colony A large group of animals or people

flint A kind of rock that is brown or dark gray in color and can break into thin, sharp flakes

improvise To find a new way to do something using only the materials or items you have with you and not the proper tools for the job

larvae The young of many insects, including ants and termites. Larvae hatch from eggs

morale The way a person or group of people feels about themselves and their abilities

predator An animal that hunts, kills, and eats other animals

prey An animal that is hunted and killed by another animal for food

sap A watery, sometimes sticky, liquid inside plants

span The measurement of something, from end to end

territory In the animal world, a territory is an area of land where an animal lives, finds its food, and its mate

venomous An animal that uses venom to kill prey or to defend itself. Venom is a poison that is deliberately passed onto a victim through a bite or sting

The eyelash pit viper hunts frogs and birds. It spends most of its time in low-hanging trees and vines. Although it is not large, 19–31 inches (48–78 centimeters), it is very poisonous! Its **venomous** bite will cause body tissue damage and could even lead to death.

The green anaconda is the world's largest snake. It can grow to 32.8 feet (ten meters) long.

It waits in water to catch **prey** such as deer. The green anaconda wraps its body around its prey to squeeze out all the air. Then it swallows its prey whole.

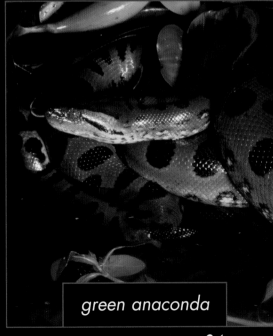

green anaconda

The black caiman is the Amazon's largest water **predator**. It can grow to 19.36 feet (six meters) long.

black caiman

The goliath bird-eating tarantula can have a leg **span** of 9.8 inches (25 centimeters). If it thinks it is in danger, it shoots out tiny hairs from its body. The hairs will irritate your skin and eyes.

goliath bird-eating tarantula

CHAPTER 6

PROTECT YOUR BODY

It is very important to stay clean in a survival situation. Dirty skin can become infected and cause illness.

Check for things living on your body every day!

Ticks will attach to your body and suck blood. Cover the tick in tree **sap**. This will cut off the tick's air supply and it will die.

tick

Leeches also attach to your body and suck blood.

Be careful not to swallow a leech. It could attach to the inside of your throat. Pull off leeches as soon as you can.

leech

CHAPTER 7

RESCUE

The jungle is a thick tangle of trees and bushes. This makes it hard for rescue planes to see you.